DON'T DO IT!

DON'T DO IT!
Warning words from
the wise and the witty

Gerd de Ley and David Potter

PRION

First published 2002 in Great Britain by
Prion Books Limited
Imperial Works, Perren Street
London NW5 3ED
www.prionbooks.com

ISBN 1-85375-492-7

Cover design by Grade Design

Printed and bound in Great Britain
by Bookmarque, Croyden, Surrey

Never take the advice of someone who has not had your kind of trouble.

SYDNEY J. HARRIS

Never give advice... Sell it!

MITCH MURRAY

Never accept a drink
from a urologist.

ERMA BOMBECK

Never accept an invitation from
a stranger unless he offers
you candy.

LINDA FESTA

Never admit to being older than
your bra size.

JOAN RIVERS

Never agree with your boss until he says something.

BRUCE W. VAN ROY

Never allow your child to call you by your first name. He hasn't known you long enough.

FRAN LEBOWITZ

Never answer a
hypothetical question.

MOSHE ARENS

Never bite the hand that
has your allowance in it.

LISA TIDLER

Never answer phones promptly.
You don't want to appear too
desperate for business.

STEVE ALTES

Never appeal to a man's 'better nature' – he might not have one.

ROBERT A. HEINLEIN

Never have sex with a man. It leads to kissing and pretty soon you've got to talk to them.

STEVE MARTIN

Never approach a bull from the front, a horse from the rear or a fool from any direction.

KEN ALSTAD

Never argue with anyone younger than yourself; they know it all.

HELEN VAN ETTEN

Never argue with a fool ... he may be doing the same thing.

Mitch Murray

Never argue with a fool – people might not know the difference.

Peter Darbo

Never argue with idiots. They will bring you down to their level, then overwhelm you with their experience.

DAVE JOHNSON

Never argue with a man who buys ink by the barrel.

BILL GREENER

Never ask a man where's he's been.
If he's out on legitimate business,
he doesn't need an alibi. And, girls,
if he has been out on illegitimate
business, it's your own fault.

MAE WEST

Never ask a man – just make
him tell you.

SIDNEY TREMAYNE

Never ask why you've been
fired, because if you do, they're
liable to tell you.

JERRY COLEMAN

Never assume that the guy
understands that you and he
have a relationship.

DAVE BARRY

Never attempt levity while filling
out your insurance forms.

W. J. VOGEL

Never attempt to teach a pig to
sing, it wastes your time and
annoys the pig.

ROBERT A. HEINLEIN

Never attribute to malice
that which can be
adequately explained by
straightforward stupidity.

JOHN CHURTON COLLINS

Never be alone in the lift with
the man who has religious
tracts in his desk.

FAITH HINES

Never be flippantly rude to
elderly strangers in foreign
hotels. They always turn out
to be the King of Sweden.

SAKI

Never be haughty to the humble.
Never be humble to the haughty.

JEFFERSON DAVIS

Don't be irreplaceable.
If you can't be replaced,
you can't be promoted.

LODE MARLEY

Don't look before you leap.
It'll ruin the surprise.

KRIS BRAND

Never be unfaithful to a lover,
except with your wife.

P. J. O'ROURKE

Never believe anything until it's
been officially denied.

ANTONY JAY AND JONATHAN LYNN

Never bet on a dead
horse or a live woman.

JIM MURRAY

Never brag about your ancestors
coming over on the Mayflower;
the immigration laws weren't as
strict in those days.

LEW LEHR

Never bet with a man
named 'One-Iron'.

Tom Sharp

Never borrow money
from your boss.

Pieter Klaas Jagersma

Never buy anything you can't lift.

JOHN BEAR

Never buy a programme.
When you want to read it,
the lights go out.

KADÉ BRUIN

Never buy a used car if the
radio buttons are all on
hard-rock stations.

MARK PATINKIN

Never call a man a fool;
borrow from him.

ADDISON MIZNER

Never change
diapers in midstream.

DON MARQUIS

Never chase a lie. Let it alone, and it will run itself to death.

Lyman Beecher

Never comment on a woman's rear end. Never use the words "large" or "size" with "rear end." Never. Avoid the area altogether. Trust me.

Tim Allen

Never complain about your troubles; they are responsible for more than half of your income.

ROBERT R. UPDEGRAFF

Never confuse brilliance with a bull market.

PAUL RUBIN

Never criticize Americans.
They have the best taste
that money can buy.

MILES KINGTON

Never cross a horse
with a loose woman.

JOHN LENNON

Never delay kissing a pretty girl
or opening a bottle of whiskey.

ERNEST HEMINGWAY

Never despise what it says in the
women's magazines: it may not be
subtle, but neither are men.

ZSA ZSA GABOR

Never dine in a restaurant where the speciality of the house is the Heimlich manoeuvre.

VICTOR LEWIS-SMITH

Never dive into an empty pool.

BRIAN URQUHART

Never divorce the boss's daughter.

STANLEY MARCUS

Never do anything that popular opinion and your own sense of right do not approve. Hire someone else to do it.

PHILANDER JOHNSON

Never do anything you wouldn't want to be caught dead doing.

JOHN CARRADINE

Never do anything yourself that others can do for you.

AGATHA CHRISTIE

Never do business with people who've got nothing to lose.

PIETER KLAAS JAGERSMA

Never do that again! For further details, consult your conscience.

ASHLEIGH BRILLIANT

Never do to yourself what
you can do to others.

J. P. GOETHUYS

Never do to others
what they do to you.

LEOPOLD KOCH

Never do unto someone else what
you want to do unto his wife.

François Cavanna

Never do today what you
can put off till tomorrow.

William Brighty Rands

Never do with your hands what you
could do better with your mouth.

Cherry Vanilla

Never doubt the courage of the French. They were the ones who discovered that snails were edible.

DOUG LARSON

Never doubt what no one is sure about.

ROALD DAHL

Never drink from your finger
bowl – it contains only water.

ADDISON MIZNER

Never drink black coffee
at lunch; it will keep you
awake in the afternoon.

JILLY COOPER

Never drink water – look
at the way it rusts pipes.

W. C. FIELDS

Never drop dead
around a specialist.

S. J. PERELMAN

Never drop your
gun to hug a bear.

H. E. PALMER

Never eat anything
bigger than your head.

B. KLIBAN

Never eat any product on which
the listed ingredients cover more
than one-third of the package.

JOSEPH LEONARD

Never eat in a restaurant that
calls itself a nightclub.

JIM QUINN

Never eat in a restaurant with a
souvenir shop attached.

JIM QUINN

Never eat in a place called Mom's.

NELSON ALGREN

Never eat prunes
when you're hungry.

ROD SCHMIDT

Never eat spaghetti
in the land of the blind.

ARNO KERKHOFS

Never eat in a restaurant
where you see a cockroach
bench-pressing a burrito.

PAT MCCORMICK

Never eat anything at
one sitting that you can't lift.

JIM HENSON

Never eat anything
you can't pronounce.

RICK MARLING

You should never end a sentence
with a preposition.

JILL ETHERINGTON

Never exaggerate your faults;
your friends will attend to that.

ROBERT C. EDWARDS

Never expect a quick answer from a pipe smoker. He will always fiddle with his pipe first. That's the real reason he smokes a pipe.

Roger Simon

Never explain. Your friends do not need it and your enemies will not believe you anyway.

Elbert Hubbard

Never expose an erogenous zone without getting the money first.

JOAN RIVERS

Never face facts; if you do you'll never get up in the morning.

MARLO THOMAS

Never fight an inanimate object.

P. J. O'ROURKE

Never feel remorse for what you have thought about your wife; she has thought much worse about you.

JEAN ROSTAND

Never be so broadminded that your brains fall out.

L. L. LEVINSON

Never fight a war unless you have been attacked and your country is in danger – or unless you are sure you can win.

ALEX AYRES

Never floss with a stranger.

JOAN RIVERS

Never follow whisky with port.

P. V. TAYLOR

Never forget what
you need to remember.

GARRETT BARTLEY

Never get deeply in debt
to someone who cried
at the end of Scarface.

ROBERT S. WIEDER

Never get a mime talking. He
won't stop.

MARCEL MARCEAU

Never get into S & M with a guy
who wears imitation leather.

JOAN RIVERS

Never get in a gun fight with
seven men when you only have a
six-shooter.

W.J. VOGEL

Never get into fights with ugly people. They have nothing to lose.

ANONYMOUS

Never describe your long-term marital ambitions on the first date.

ABBY HIRSCH

Never get into an argument with a schizophrenic person and say, "Who do you think you are?"

RAY COMBS

Never get into a pissing contest with a skunk.

ARTHUR BAER

Never get into a narrow double bed with a wide single man.

QUENTIN CRISP

Never get into a car with
bucket seats – unless there's
champagne in the buckets.

JOAN RIVERS

Never get married in the morning,
'cause you may never know who
you'll meet that night.

PAUL HORNUNG

Never get the 12.50 train. It's only ten to one you'll catch it.

Tony Blackburn

Never give a sucker an even break.

W. C. Fields

Never get your flat tire fixed by a guy who's chewing gum.

Johnny Hart

Never give a party if you will be the most interesting person there.

MICKEY FRIEDMAN

Never get up before breakfast. If you have to get up before breakfast, eat breakfast first.

TEXAS BIX BENDER

Never go to bed mad.
Stay up and fight.

PHYLLIS DILLER

Never go out with a man who
wears tight jeans because if he's
comfortable in them there will be
nothing in them to interest you.

LIZ HUGHES

Never go to a doctor whose office plants have died.

ERMA BOMBECK

Never grow up completely, because that is when you start getting old.

ROGER CLINTON

Never hide your preferences. Maybe they are already old-fashioned.

WIESLAW BRUDZINSKI

Never hire an electrician whose eyebrows are scorched.

MASON WILDER

Never have children, only grandchildren.

GORE VIDAL

People spend too much time
waiting in lines. There are two
things you should never have to
wait in line to do: one is to go to
the bathroom; the other is
to make love.

ALEX AYRES

Never hire who you can't fire.

ERIC REID

Never hit a man when he's down.
Kick him. It's much easier.

Milton Berle

Never hit a man with glasses. Hit
him with a baseball bat.

Anonymous

Never hold discussions with the
monkey when the organ grinder
is in the room.

Winston Churchill

Never hunt rabbit with dead dog.

EARL DERR BIGGERS

Never insult an alligator until after you have crossed the river.

CORDELL HULL

Never insult anyone by accident.

ROBERT A. HEINLEIN

Never interrupt when
you are being flattered.

Daniel Boorstin

Never introduce the
Vice-President of the company
you work for as the boss's wife.

Kay Chirichigno

Never invest in anything
that eats or needs repainting.

Billy Rose

Never invite a cannibal to a picnic.

JOSÉ ARTUR

Never itch for anything you
aren't willing to scratch for.

IVERN BALL

Never judge a book by its cover.

FRAN LEBOWITZ

Never judge a book
by its cover price.

PHILIP J. FRANKENFELD

Never keep up with the Joneses.
Drag them down to your level,
it's cheaper.

QUENTIN CRISP

Never kick a fresh
turd on a hot day.

HARRY S. TRUMAN

Never kill an ass who may have
to lay a golden egg.

FREDERICK LONSDALE

Never kick a man when he is up.

TIP O'NEILL

Never laugh at live dragons.

J. R. R. TOLKIEN

Never lend any money to anybody
unless they don't need it.

OGDEN NASH

Never knock on Death's door.
Ring the bell and run away.
Death really hates that.

MATT FREWER

Never laugh at a limping
general. A man with a short leg
may have a long arm.

CLEM SCHOUWENAARS

Never lend books, for no one ever
returns them. The only books I
have in my library are books that
other folks have leant me.

ANATOLE FRANCE

Never lend your car to anyone to
whom you have given birth.

ERMA BOMBECK

Never let a drunk friend drive –
especially if the party was
at his place.

LARRY M. SLAVENS

Never let a fool kiss you,
or a kiss fool you.

JOEY ADAMS

Never let a guy get away with kissing you on the first date if you can get him to do more.

JOAN RIVERS

Never let modesty stand in the way of the facts.

PAUL B. LOWNEY

Never let a panty line show around your ankles.

JOAN RIVERS

Never let the facts interfere with your story.

DAVID S. GRUBNICK

Never let a gift horse in the house.

LEO ROSTEN

Never let anything mechanical
know you are in a hurry.

ANDREW ROSS

Never let them do to us what we
would do to them if they let us.

ASHLEIGH BRILLIANT

Never let your fear of God
keep you out of heaven.

MERRIT MALLOY

Never let your sense of
morals prevent you from
doing what's right.

Isaac Asimov

Never let your career
interfere with your hobbies.

Steve Altes

Never let your mind get set –
except on the objective of
succeeding by exercising an
open mind.

ROBERT HELLER

Never lie, always exaggerate.

ERIC PISCADOR

Never look backwards or you'll
fall down the stairs.

RUDOLF NUREYEV

Never look up a word
you cannot spell.

GARY O. BALUSEK

Never spell a word
you cannot look up.

GARY O. BALUSEK

Never lose an opportunity
to jump ship.

Arthur Wallesley

Rule No.1: Never lose money.
Rule No. 2: Never forget Rule No.1.

Warren Buffett

Never make a task of pleasure, as
the man said when he dug his
wife's grave only three feet deep.

Seamus MacManus

Never make love on a Saturday evening, otherwise you won't know what to do if it rains on Sunday.

Lucien Guitry

Never make forecasts, especially about the future.

Samuel Goldwyn

Never make love in
a suit of armor.

MICHAEL GREEN

Never make passes at
men with full glasses.

JASMINE BIRTLES

Never make the mistake of
assuming the critters will
beat a path to your door.

JOHN P. MASCOTTE

Never make the same mistake
twice, unless it pays.

MAE WEST

Never marry a widow unless her
first husband was hanged.

JAMES KELLY

Never marry a woman who has an extensive knowledge of nautical terms and can tie over 200 knots.

Lewis Grizzard

Never marry a widow whose first husband was poisoned.

Texas Bix Bender and Gladiola Montana

Never marry a woman who carries a coin changer on her belt.

Lewis Grizzard

Never marry for money. You can borrow it a lot cheaper.

ANN LANDERS

Never miss a chance to have sex or appear on television.

GORE VIDAL

Never miss a chance to
keep your mouth shut.

Robert Newton Peck

Never mistake asthma
for passion and vice versa.

Anjanette Comer

Never mistake a clear
view for a short distance.

Paul Saffo

Never moon a werewolf.

MIKE BINDER

Never trust a sane person.

LYLE ALZADO

Never murder a man who is committing suicide.

WOODROW WILSON

Never offend people with style
when you can offend them
with substance.

SAM BROWN

Never negotiate with a bastard –
just smack him in the face.

GERARD COX

Never offend either a publicist or a trombone player. If you get on the wrong side of either of them, you're fucked.

ROSALEEN LINEHAN

Never name a movie character "Joe".

WILLIAM FLANAGAN

Never offer someone
both your hands.

KAREL BOULLART

Never open a box
you didn't close.

MIKE BERMAN

Never order a drink where
you get to keep the glass.

ROGER SIMON

Never order bratwurst in a
Chinese restaurant.

JIM QUINN

Never overestimate the
intelligence of the voter.

H. L. MENCKEN

It is never wise to
overestimate lawyers.

LISA SCOTTOLINE

Never pass a snow plow
on the right.

GREGORY SINGLETON

Never place a large bet
on a game you lose.

CHRIS TUCKER

Never play computer games with
children or teenagers, unless you
enjoy being humiliated.

MIKE KNOWLES

Never play poker with a
man called Ace.

LINDSEY NELSON

Never play cards with
a man called Doc.

NELSON ALGREN

Never play cards with a man with
dark glasses or his own deck.

JIM MURRAY

Never play cat and mouse
games if you're a mouse.

DON ADDIS

Never play Russian roulette,
you will always lose.

DANIEL VADET

Never postpone until
tomorrow what you should
have done yesterday.

ALEXANDER POLA

Never play leapfrog with a unicorn.

ANONYMOUS

Never practice two vices at once.

TALLULAH BANKHEAD

Never pray for justice,
because you might get some.

MARGARET ATWOOD

Never pray for money.
The Lord is your shepherd,
not your banker.

ROBERT ORBEN

Never program and drink
beer at the same time.

B. D. WOLTMAN

Never purchase beauty products
in a hardware store.

JIM HENSON

Never put an iced doughnut
on a mouse pad.

RICHARD MORAN

Never put a smoke alarm
between your thighs.

JOAN RIVERS

Never put a sock in a toaster.

Eddie Izzard

Never put anything on paper, my boy, and never trust a man with a small black moustache.

P. G. Wodehouse

Never put off for tomorrow who you can put out for tonight.

JOAN RIVERS

Never question your wife's judgement. Look at who she married.

R. GREER

Never raise your hand to your children; it leaves your groin unprotected.

RED BUTTONS

Never regard as accurate a policy
decision flow chart with more
than one feedback loop.

MARTIN H. WEISS

Never reheat a soufflé.

PAUL MCCARTNEY

Never remember what
you can afford to forget.

ANDREW S. HASSELBRING

Never resist a mad impulse
to do something nice for me.

ASHLEIGH BRILLIANT

Never review the troops until you
know whose troops they are.

D. H. LEE

Never ruin an apology
with an excuse.

KIMBERLY JOHNSON

Never run into debt, not if you can find anything else to run into.

JOSH BILLINGS

Never say anything in front of a child, however young, that can subsequently be used against you.

FAITH HINES

Never say "Hi Jack" in an Airport.

TERRY DENTON

Never say "never" and
always avoid "always".

JOHN M. HAZLITT

Never say anything remarkable.
It is sure to be wrong.

MARK RUTHERFORD

Never say "Oops" in
the operating theatre.

LEO TROY

Never say famous last words.
They could be.

BILLY CRYSTAL

Never say you don't know – nod wisely, leave calmly, then run like hell to find an expert.

SANDRA ODDO

Never jump on a man unless he's down.

FINLEY PETER DUNNE

Never serve oysters in a month that has no paycheck in it.

P. J. O'ROURKE

Never settle with words
what you can accomplish
with a flamethrower.

BRUCE FEIRSTEIN

Never smack a man
who's chewing tobacco.

TEXAS BIX BENDER

Never sleep three in a bed – or you'll wake up three in a bed.

GÜNTER GRASS

Never sleep with a woman whose troubles are worse than your own.

NELSON ALGREN

Never sleep with a man who fakes foreplay.

JASMINE BIRTLES

Never sleep with a
fat man in July.

MODINE GUNCH

Never shout for help during
the night. You might wake
your neighbours.

STANISLAW JERZY LEC

Never show the audience
something they can imagine
better than you can show it.

BILL DOUGLAS

Never sigh into a container
of goldfish flakes.

KELLY MILLAR

Never speak loudly to one another
unless the house is on fire.

H. W. THOMPSON

Never stand between
a dog and the hydrant.

JOHN PEERS

Never start a project until you've
picked out someone to blame.

JOHNNY HART AND BRANT PARKER

Never start before you are ready.

JULIET AWON-UIBOPUU

Never steal anything so small that you'll have to go to an unpleasant city jail instead of a minimum security federal tennis prison.

P. J. O'ROURKE

Never stow away on a Kamikaze plane.

T. R. M. SPENCE

Never take a cross country
trip with a kid who has just
learned to whistle.

JEAN DEUEL

Never take an out-of-state check.

JOAN RIVERS

Never take your eye
off a cow's arse.

JACQUES CHIRAC

Never take a punch at a
man named Sullivan.

H. ALLEN SMITH

Never take vacations
To visit relations.

GERALD BARZAN

Never take a reference from a clergyman. They always want to give someone a second chance.

LADY SELBORNE

Never take a tip from a guy eating in a luncheonette.

DAN JENKINS

Never tell a lie... unless lying is one of your strong points.

GEORGE WASHINGTON PLUNKITT

You can tell a person they're ugly. You can tell a person their feet smell. You can even insult their mother, but never, never, never tell them they're stupid.

JEROME G. GANCI

Never tell the truth to those
unworthy of it...

MARK TWAIN

Never tell anyone your dreams.
Maybe Freud's followers will
come to power.

STANISLAW JERZY LEC

Two Great Rules of Life:
Never tell everything at once.

Ken Venturi

Never thank anybody for
anything, except for a drink
of water in the desert –
and then make it brief.

Gene Fowler

Never think you can
lose both gloves.

W. J. VOGEL

Never throw a stone at a woman,
unless it's a precious one.

JEAN-GABRIEL DOMERGUE

Never throw stones at your mother,
You'll be sorry for it when she's
dead. Never throw stones at your
mother, Throw bricks at your father
instead.

BRENDAN BEHAN

Never trust a naked milkman.

JASMINE BIRTLES

Never trust or love anyone so
much you can't betray him.

MARK TWAIN

Never trust your friends,
they are the nearest to you.
When they stab they won't miss.

LUC HUYBRECHTS

Never trust love at first sight –
take a second look.

JASMINE BIRTLES

Never trust a man who combs his
hair straight from his left armpit.

ALICE ROOSEVELT LONGWORTH

Never trust anybody who says
"trust me". Except just this
once, of course.

JOHN VARLEY

Never trust a man who, when he's alone in a room with a tea cosy doesn't try it on.

BILLY CONNOLLY

Never trust a man with short legs – brains too near their bottoms.

NOEL COWARD

Never trust a round garter or a
Wall Street man.

DOROTHY PARKER

Never trust a sister over twelve.

STEPHEN ROOS

Never trust a husband too
far or a bachelor too near.

HELEN ROWLAND

One should never trust a woman
who tells one her real age. A
woman who would tell one that,
would tell one anything.

OSCAR WILDE

Never trust a computer you
can't throw out a window.

STEPHEN WOZNIAK

Never trust the food in a restaurant on top of the tallest building in town that spends a lot of time folding napkins.

ANDY ROONEY

Never trust a man who looks like he walks down Lovers Lane holding his own hand.

FRED ALLEN

Never trust anyone over thirty.

JACK WEINBERG

Never trust anyone over 30
who used to say "Never trust
anyone over 30." Never trust
anyone over-dirty.

ROBERT BYRNE

Never try to smash a lawyer in the face. You might hurt yourself.

PETE FERGUSON

Never try to be nice to a man with a tattoo on his face.

PAUL DICKSON

Never, never try anything that looks like vomit.

JEAN KERR

Never try to tell everything
you know. It may take too
short a time.

NORMAN FORD

Never try to photograph music.

JAN-WALTER DE NEVE

Never try to set an iceberg on fire.

MARCEL ACHARD

Kids, you tried your best and you failed miserably. The lesson is, never try.

MATT GROENING

Never try to explain computers to a layman. It's easier to explain sex to a virgin.

ROBERT HEINLEIN

Never try to lick ice-cream
off a hot sidewalk.

CHARLES SCHULZ

Never try to walk across a river
just because it has an average
depth of four feet.

MILTON FRIEDMAN

Never try to outstubborn a cat.

ROBERT A. HEINLEIN

Never try to wear a hat that has
more character than you do.

LANCE MORROW

Never turn your back on
the javelin competition.

DWIGHT STONES

Never under any circumstances write comedy for laughs. This is as ruinous as believing that your wife means it when she says: "Tell me all about her. I swear I don't mind."

Hugh Leonard

Never underestimate a child's ability to get into more trouble.

Martin Mull

Never underestimate the stupidity
of the general public.

SCOTT ADAMS

Never underestimate the capacity
of another human being to have
exactly the same shortcomings
you have.

LEIGH STEINBERG

Never underestimate
the hazards of a zipper.

JOAN RIVERS

Never underestimate anything.
Once the fate of humanity
depended on an apple.

LEOPOLD KOCH

Never underestimate the effectiveness of a straight cash bribe.

CLAUD COCKBURN

Never underestimate a man who overestimates himself.

FRANKLIN D. ROOSEVELT

Never underestimate the power of human stupidity.

ROBERT HEINLEIN

Never underestimate the
power of a platitude.

EDGAR R. FIEDLER

Never underestimate the
power of very stupid people
in large groups.

JOHN KENNETH GALBRAITH

Never underestimate the power
of the irate customer.

JOEL E. ROSS AND MICHAEL J. KAMI

Never underestimate your
opponent. Never take what he
offers you.

MICHAEL CRICHTON

Never wear anything that leaves
something to the imagination.

JOAN RIVERS

Never undress in front
of a bearded lady.

Evan Esar

Never underestimate the band-
width of a station wagon full of
tapes hurtling down the highway.

A. A. Tannenbaum

Never use a big word when
a little filthy one will do.

JOHNNY CARSON

Never use a jumping pole that
is longer than the height of
the jump.

ALEXANDER POLA

Never wear designer shields.

JOAN RIVERS

Never use your thumb for a rule.
You'll either hit it with a hammer
or get a splinter in it.

EDWARD KARL

Never vote for the best candidate,
vote for the one who will do the
least harm.

FRANK DANE

Never wear handcuffs with plaid.

JOAN RIVERS

Never vote for anyone; always vote against.

W. C. FIELDS

Never walk so fast that no one can come up with you.

GYS MIEDEMA

Never watch anything
stupider than you.

BETTE MIDLER

Never wear any latex or rubber
undergarment except for
recreational purposes.

JOAN RIVERS

Never wear anything that panics
the cat.

P. J. O'ROURKE

Never work for a boss who
opens the company mail.

BETTY JOE BYARS

Never wrestle with
a chimney sweep.

HERBERT H. ASQUITH

Never wrestle a pig. You both get dirty and only the pig likes it.

GREGORY SINGLETON

Never wear Odor-Eaters any place but in your shoes.

JOAN RIVERS

Never let your yearnings get
ahead of your earnings.

TEXAS BIX BENDER

Never learn to do anything. If you
don't learn you'll always find
someone else to do it.

JAME CLEMENS

Never refer to your wedding night
as the "original amateur hour".

PHYLLIS DILLER

Never get your knickers in a knot.
Nothing is solved and it just
makes you walk funny.

KATHRYN CARPENTER

Never take advice from people
with missing fingers.

Henry Beard

Never allow your children to mix
the drinks. It is unseemly and
they use too much vermouth.

Fran Lebowitz

Never come crawling to a man
for love – he likes to get
a run for his money.

MAE WEST

Don't blame God;
He's only human.

LEO ROSTEN

Never enjoy encounter groups. If you enjoy being made to feel inadequate, call your mother.

LIZ SMITH

Never expect a stranger to wipe your nose.

CYNTHIA COPELAND LEWIS

Never leave things unfinishe

DONALD R. WOODS

Never meddle in the affairs of cats, for they are subtle and will piss on your computer.

ELISABETH RIBA

Don't take life too seriously. You'll never get out alive.

TEX AVERY

Never talk about yourself; it will be done when you leave.

ADDISON MIZNER

Never touch a woman's knee at the dinner table. She has an instinctive knowledge whether a man who touches her knee is caressing her or only wiping his greasy fingers on her stocking.

GEORGE MOORE

Never trust a brilliant idea
unless it survives the hangover.

JIMMY BRESLIN

Don't try diving for the first time
in front of a bunch of people.

CYNTHIA COPELAND LEWIS

Never shear the sheep that laid the golden egg that is going to cause the well to run dry.

MORRIS UDALL

Never try to cut your own hair.

WINSTON GROOM

Never worry about avoiding temptation. As you grow older, it starts avoiding you.

PETER DARBO

Never do anything you wouldn't be willing to explain on television.

ARJAY MILLER

Never take down another man's fence.

TEXAS BIX BENDER

Never go in if you don't
know the way out.

TEXAS BIX BENDER

Never supply the rocks that
are to be thrown at you.

GENE DALY

Don't marry a man to reform
him – that's what reform
schools are for.

MAE WEST

Don't ever get your speedometer confused with your clock, like I did once, because the faster you go the later you think you are.

JACK HANDEY

Don't worry if you're a kleptomaniac, you can always take something for it.

ROBERT BENCHLEY

Never be more ridiculous
than nature made you.

C. BUDDINGH

Don't bother going to the
chiropractor to get rid of a pain
in the neck. Just divorce him.

JASMINE BIRTLES

Don't forget to tell
everyone it's a secret.

GERALD F. LIEBERMAN

Don't carry a grudge. While you're carrying the grudge, the other guy's out dancing.

BUDDY HACKETT

Don't fly on an airline where the pilots believe in reincarnation.

SPALDING GRAY

Don't hoover under your husband's feet – it's grounds for divorce.

JILLY COOPER

Don't ignore your child's bizarre behaviour – it could be symptomatic of a disorder called growing up.

ASHLEIGH BRILLIANT

Don't just do something,
stand there.

DEAN ACHESON

Don't meet trouble halfway.
It is quite capable of making
the entire journey.

STANISLAW JERZY LEC

Do not take things to
be as tragic as they are.

KARL VALENTIN

Don't nod on the phone.

CYNTHIA COPELAND LEWIS

Don't worry about the world
coming to an end today. It's
already tomorrow in Australia.

CHARLES SCHULZ

Other humorous quotation books by Prion:
Des MacHale
Wit
Wit Hits The Spot
Wit On Target
Wit – The Last Laugh
Wit Rides Again

Aubrey Malone
The Cynic's Dictionary

Michelle Lovric
Women's Wicked Wit

Rosemarie Jarski
Hollywood Wit

Look out for:

Michael Powell
High Society
Funny Money

PRION HUMOUR

Get ready to laugh yourself silly with these upcoming great titles from the Prion Humour list:

☞ The World's Worst Poetry

What happens when poetry goes wrong and how bad can it get? Stephen Robins has scoured anthologies to collect together for the first time the most delightful examples of truly awful poetry.

☛ How To Get Famous

If you think getting famous is all about tits and teeth ... you're probably right. Find out all about the machiavellian machinations behind the surface glamour of fame, and how you can play dirty along with the best of them. You might end up a drug-addled, bloated egomaniac ... but it'll be worth it. You'll be a celebrity!

☛ Toast – homage to a superfood

Why don't we all just admit it? We don't give a toss about sun-dried tomatoes or seared tuna.

What the nation really craves is toast. Funnier than Delia Smith and with more recipes than *Longitude*, TOAST tells you everything you need to know about the nation's favourite food.

Find out about other Prion humour titles at:

www.prionbooks.com